Around the World

Let's Visit Greece

Susie Brooks

PowerKiDS press

New York

Published in 2010 by The Rosen Publishing Group Inc.
29 East 21st Street, New York, NY 10010

First Edition

Library of Congress Cataloging-in-Publication Data

Brooks, Susie.
  Let's visit Greece / Susie Brooks.
    p. cm. -- (Around the world)
  Includes index.
  ISBN 978-1-4358-3028-8 (library binding)
  ISBN 978-1-4358-8610-0 (paperback)
  ISBN 978-1-4358-8611-7 (6-pack)
  1. Greece--Description and travel--Juvenile literature.
  2. Greece--Juvenile literature. I. Title.
  DF728.B765 2010
  914.9504'76--dc22

                          2008051884

Manufactured in China

Note to parents and teachers

The projects and activities in this book
are designed to be completed by children.
However, we recommend adult supervision
at all times since the Publisher cannot be
held responsible for any injury caused
while completing the projects.

Web Sites

Due to the changing nature of Internet
links, PowerKids Press has developed
an online list of Web sites related to
the subject of this book. This site
is updated regularly. Please use this
link to access this list:
www.powerkidslinks.com/world/greece

Picture Credits
p5: © Joyce Bentley; p6: © Geoff du Feu/Alamy; p7: © Jennie Hart/Alamy; p8, title page: © Todd A. Gipstein/Corbis;
p9: © Barry Lewis/Corbis; p10: © Walter Bibikow/JAI/Corbis; p11: © Silwen Randebrock/Alamy; p12: © Daniella
Nowitz/Corbis; p13: © Jon Hicks/Corbis; p14: © Werner Otto/Alamy; p15: © imagebroker/Alamy; p16: © Danita
Delimont/Alamy; p17: © FAN travelstock/Alamy; p18: © Peter M. Wilson/Alamy; p19: © Rod Edwards/Alamy; p20:
© Dave Bartruff/Corbis; p21: © Dorling Kindersley; p22: © Edward Parker/Alamy; p23: © Kuttig—Travel/Alamy; p24:
© James Davis Photography/Alamy; p25: © Owen Franken/Corbis; p26: © Jack Carey/Alamy; p27: © IML Image Group
Ltd/Alamy; p28: © Roger Cracknell 01/classic/Alamy; p29: © IML Image Group Ltd/Alamy; Rita Storey/Wishlist; p31:
© Greek School.

Cover: Tourists on the Acropolis in Athens © Daniella Nowitz/Corbis; Greek food Dave © Bartruff/Corbis.

Contents

This is Greece!

Greece is a hilly country in southeast Europe. It sticks out into the sea and includes many islands. The easiest way to get here is by airplane.

Greece has lots of places to visit—this book will show you a few.

Many people choose just one Greek island for their vacation. Others travel around. Wherever you go, you will notice things that are different from home.

The Greek language has its own alphabet—the bottom half of this sign is written in it.

We raced to be first to see the sea. I saw it from the plane window!

Speak Greek!

hi
giásou (yah-sou)
yes
né (neh)
no
óhi (oh-hee)

Summer hotspot

Greece is a popular place for summer vacations. The weather is hot and sunny, and you are never far from the sea.

Greece has lots of sandy beaches. This one is on the island of Antipaxos.

The middle of the day was hottest— we sat under a beach umbrella to keep out of the sun.

July and August can be sweltering and very busy! June and September are good times to visit. In the winter, most of Greece is cool and rainy.

It's important to put on plenty of sunscreen to stop your skin from burning.

Speak Greek!

beach
paralîa (pa-ra-**lee**-ya)
hot
zestó (zess-**toh**)
cold
kryó (kree-**yoh**)

7

Cool houses

Near the Greek seaside there are many hotels, **villas**, and **apartments** to stay in. They may have a swimming pool and patios for sunbathing.

Some hotels have a pool on the roof!

I found a little lizard running up my bedroom wall! Dad said it was a gecko.

Houses are stacked high in the hillside village of Oia on Santorini island.

Many Greek villages are built on hillsides. The houses are made of stone and are often painted white to keep them cool inside.

Handy gadgets

- Mosquito repellent plug—to keep biting insects away!
- Plug adapter—the wall sockets are different in Greece.
- Mini-fan—to keep you cool!

All aboard!

Huge ferries take people and cars to the larger islands.

You will probably go on a boat at some point during your vacation—especially if you visit an island.

Speak Greek!

bus
leoforío (lay-o-for-**ee**-yo)

taxi
taksí (tack-**see**)

passenger boat
plîo (pl**ee**-yoh)

Greek roads can be winding, and many towns and villages have narrow streets. Scooters and motorcycles are popular ways to get around.

The tiny island of Hydra has no cars. Instead, people use donkeys or **mules**.

There were big waves when we went on the ferry—everything rocked and I felt seasick!

Exciting Athens

Athens is the capital of Greece. One sight everyone wants to see here is the Parthenon— an ancient temple on a hill called the Acropolis.

It's a long climb up the Acropolis, but worth it—wear sturdy shoes!

People said the Parthenon changed color in the evening light—and it really did!

You get a great view of the city from the Parthenon. Around the ancient parts of Athens, the streets are lively and modern.

You can watch the changing of the guard in Syntagma Square.

Things to do...

Run around in the National Gardens

Go back in time at the Children's Museum

Take a train up inside Lykavitos Hill

13

A trip back in time

Imagine living in ancient Greece, thousands of years ago! Wherever you go, look for clues like these...

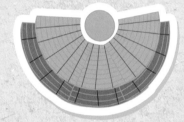

Theaters
The **ancient Greeks** loved watching a show.

You can still sit on the seats at the Epidauros theater.

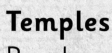

Temples

People worshipped lots of gods in ancient **temples**. There is a famous one in Delphi.

This is the throne room of King Minos in the palace of Knossos, on the island of Crete.

Palaces

Grand palaces were built for ancient Greek kings. The walls have crumbled over the years, but you can still see treasures inside!

15

Island worlds

You would need a lot of time to explore all the Greek islands—there are thousands. However, people don't live on them all. Each island is special in its own way.

Fishing is a big part of life on many Greek islands.

Some people go on sailing trips around groups of islands. With a boat, you can reach beaches that no one else can get to.

If you go to Mykonos, you might meet the local hero—Petros the pelican!

Island fun

Corfu—swim in clear blue sea

Kos—find beaches with white or black sand

Rhodes—see a real castle and build one on the beach

17

On the rocks

Away from the coast, much of Greece is made up of mountains. These are great places for walking, climbing, river rafting, and watching wildlife.

Mountain goats are some of the best climbers in Greece!

I saw a snake—it didn't bite me, but it made me jump!

In the Meteora area in central Greece, **monasteries** mysteriously perch on tall towers of rock.

Monks still live up here—you can visit them, if you can figure out how!

Shy animals to look for

- wolves
- brown bears
- lynx (wild cats)

19

Greek feasts

You'll find all your favorite food in Greece, but don't be afraid to try new things! Greek food is colorful and tasty.

Greeks eat a healthy diet of salad with olive oil, bread, and lots of fish and seafood.

I got sticky eating souvlaki—you wrap up meat and salad in a yummy pocket of pita bread.

For breakfast, you might have Greek yogurt with honey from local bees. Crispy cheese pies or pitta bread with dips make good snacks.

On the menu

horiátiki (o-ree-a-tee-kee)
Greek salad with feta cheese, tomatoes, olives

moussaka (moo-**sah**-ka)
creamy eggplant and meat pie

baklava (ba-**klah**-va)
sticky honey and nut pastry

Time to shop

Not all Greek villages have stores, so you might need to travel to find one. Many people buy their food in local markets.

Do you like olives? You'll find plenty of them grown and sold in Greece!

If you want to buy a **souvenir** to take home, look for handmade crafts or something that reminds you of your vacation. You'll need to change your money to euros.

Natural sponges from the bottom of the sea are cheap presents to buy for friends back home.

Presents to buy

Colorful rugs and cloths

Painted pots and plates

Olive oil made from olives

Local life

Nothing happens in a hurry in Greece, so get ready to relax! The Greek people love sitting and chatting, snoozing in the afternoon, and staying up late.

You will often see Greek families sitting on their doorsteps on village streets.

This priest is preparing to baptize a child in a Greek Orthodox Church.

Most Greek people are members of the **Orthodox Church**. Children are named after saints, and they celebrate their saint's day as well as their birthday.

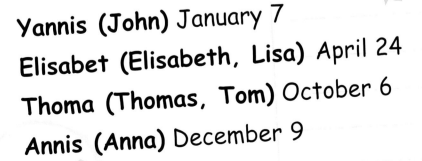

Celebrate a name

Yannis (John) January 7

Elisabet (Elisabeth, Lisa) April 24

Thoma (Thomas, Tom) October 6

Annis (Anna) December 9

Great games

In 2004, thousands of people came to Athens to watch the **Olympic Games**. The first Olympics were held here more than 2,000 years ago!

You can still run on the track at the ancient Olympic site.

Sports are very popular in Greece, especially soccer. The seaside is great for volleyball as well as swimming, windsurfing, and other water sports.

Parasailing is as good as flying! You land with a splash in the sea.

It was fun flying a kite with some Greek children on the beach.

Fun celebrations

If you come to Greece in February, look for Apokries. This is the Greek carnival that happens before **Lent**. It's a time for big parties and costume parades.

During Apokries, the islanders of Skyros dance in traditional clothes.

Cracking red eggs is an Easter tradition. If yours stays whole, you'll get good luck!

Easter is one of the biggest festivals in Greece. People celebrate with church ceremonies, candle lighting, family feasts, and games.

Make a date

~~January 1~~ look for a coin in your Vasilopitta cake—you'll be lucky all year!	~~March 25~~ watch soldiers march in big Independence Day parades.		

Play it yourself

Pretend to be an athlete in the first Olympic Games! In ancient times, only men were allowed to compete, but girls can play this, too!

The ancient Greeks used to run races on foot as part of the Olympics, just like we do now.

You will need:

- a large outdoor space
- sticks or markers
- a frisbee
- a long tape measure.

Event 1: Discus

Mark a spot to stand on. Throw the frisbee as far as you can. Measure the distance from the standing spot to the frisbee. Take turns and see whose throw is the longest.

Event 2: Chariot race

Mark a start and finish point. Line up in pairs and have a wheelbarrow race. The person on their hands is the horse—neigh all the way!

Event 3: Long jump

Mark a take-off point. Run up to it and then jump as far as you can. Measure the distance and see who jumps farthest.

Prizes

Crown your winners with **wreaths** made from real or paper leaves stuck to a hairband.

TIP: Invent other fun events. Ancient Greeks ran with shields and helmets—you could make your own!

Useful words and further information

ancient Greeks	The people who lived in Greece and other parts of Europe thousands of years ago.
apartment	A room or rooms for living in.
Lent	The 40 days leading up to Easter when Christians traditionally give something up.
monastery	A place where monks live a religious lifestyle.
mule	A cross between a donkey and a horse.
Olympic Games	The worldwide sports contest that happens every four years and first began in ancient Greece.
Orthodox Church	The main religious group in Greece and many other Eastern European countries.
souvenir	Something you take home to remind you of somewhere you have been.
taverna	A Greek restaurant.
temple	A building for worshiping gods in.
villa	A home in the countryside.
wreath	A ring of leaves or flowers. Ancient Greeks wore wreaths made from olive branches.

Books to read

A-Z: Greece by Byron Augustin (Children's Press, 2006)

Country Explorers: Greece by Madeline Donaldson (Lerner Publications, 2009)

Greece by Patrick Ryan (Child's World, 2003)

Welcome to Greece by Meredith Costain (Chelsea House Publications, 2001)